eBook - Basics of Computers

By:

Dr (Er) Om Prakash
Professor
SMS Lucknow

Introduction

All computer perform the following basic operations for converting raw input data into useful information and presenting it to the user. Five basic operations performed by computer are: Inputting, Storing, Processing, Outputting &controlling. A computer can process data, pictures, sound and graphics complicated problems quickly and accurately. Computers need to receive data and instruction in order to solve any problem. Therefore, we need to input the data and instructions into the computers. The input unit consists of one or more input devices.

A COMPUTER CAN PROCESS DATA, PICTURES, SOUND AND GRAPHICS COMPLICATED. Computers need to receive data and instruction in order to solve any problem. Therefore we need to input the data and instructions into the computers. The input unit consists of one or more input devices. Keyboard is the one of the most commonly used input device. Other commonly used input devices are the mouse, floppy disk drive, magnetic tape, etc. All the input devices perform the following functions: Accept the data and instructions from the outsideworld, Convert it to a form that the computer can understand. Supply the converted data to the computer system for further processing.

STORAGE UNIT: The storage unit of the computer holds data and instructions that are entered through the input unit, before they are processed. It preserves the intermediate and final results before these are sent to the output devices. It also saves the data for the later use.

The various storage devices of a computer system are divided into two categories.

1.   **Primary Storage:** Stores and provides very fast. This memory is generally used to hold the program being currently executed in the computer, the data being received from the input unit, the intermediate and final results of the program. The primary memory is temporary in nature. The data is lost, when the computer is switched off.

In order to store the data permanently, the data has to be transferred to the secondary memory.

The cost of the primary storage is

more compared to the secondary

storage.

Therefore most computers have limited primary storage capacity.

2. <u>Secondary Storage:</u>

Secondary storage is used like an archive. It stores several programs, documents, data bases etc. The programs that you run on the computer are first transferred to the primary memory before it is actually run. Whenever the results are saved, again they get stored in the secondary memory. The secondary memory is slower and cheaper than the primary memory. Some of the commonly used secondary memory devices are Hard disk, CD, etc..

Memory Size

All digital computers use the binary system, i.e. 0's and 1's. Each

character or a number is represented by an 8 bit code.

The set of 8 bits is called a byte. A character occupies 1

byte space. A numeric occupies 2 byte space.

Byte is the space occupied in the memory.

The size of the primary storage is specified in KB (Kilobytes) or MB (Megabyte). One KB is equal to 1024 bytes and one MB is equal to 1000KB. The size of the primary storage in a typical PC usually starts at 16MB. PCs having 32 MB, 48MB, 128 MB, 256MB memory are quite common.

Output Unit

The output unit of a computer provides the information and results of a computation to outside world.

Printers, Visual Display Unit (VDU) are the commonly used output devices.

<u>Other commonly used output devices are</u>

- ☐ floppy disk drive,

- ☐ hard disk drive, magnetic tape drive.

ARITHMETIC LOGICAL UNIT

All calculations are performed in the Arithmetic Logic Unit (ALU) of the computer.

It also does comparison and takes decision. The ALU can perform basic operations such as addition, subtraction, multiplication, division, etc and does logic operations like, >, <, =, 'etc. Whenever calculations are required, the control unit transfers the data from storage unit to ALU, once the computations are done, the results are transferred to the storage unit by the control unit and then it is send to the output unit for displaying results.

CONTROL UNIT

It controls all other units in the computer. The control unit instructs the input unit, where to store the data after receiving it from the user. It controls the flow of data and instructions from the storage unit to ALU. It also controls the flow of results from the ALU to the storage unit. The control unit is generally referred as the central nervous system of the computer that control and synchronizes its working.

CENTRAL PROCESSING UNIT

The control unit and ALU of the computer are together known as the Central Processing Unit (CPU).

The CPU is like brain performs the following functions:

- It performs all calculations.

- It takes all decisions.

- It controls all units of the computer.

A PC may have CPU-IC such as Intel 8088, 80286, 80386, 80486, Celeron, Pentium, Pentium Pro, Pentium II, Pentium III, Pentium IV, Dual Core, and AMD etc

Memory Hierarchy

The memory unit is an essential component in any digital computer since it is needed for storing programs and data. Not all accumulated information is needed by the CPU at the same time. Therefore, it is more economical to use low-cost storage devices to serve as a backup for storing the information that is not currently used by CPU.

The memory unit that directly communicate with CPU is called the main memory. Devices that provide backup storage are called auxiliary memory. The memory hierarchy system consists of all storage devices employed in a computer system from the slow by high- capacity auxiliary memory to a relatively faster main memory, to an even smaller and faster cache memory

The main memory occupies a central position by being able to communicate directly with the CPU and with auxiliary memory devices through an I/O processor

A special very-high-speed memory called cache is used to increase the speed of processing by making current programs and data available to the CPU at a rapid rate

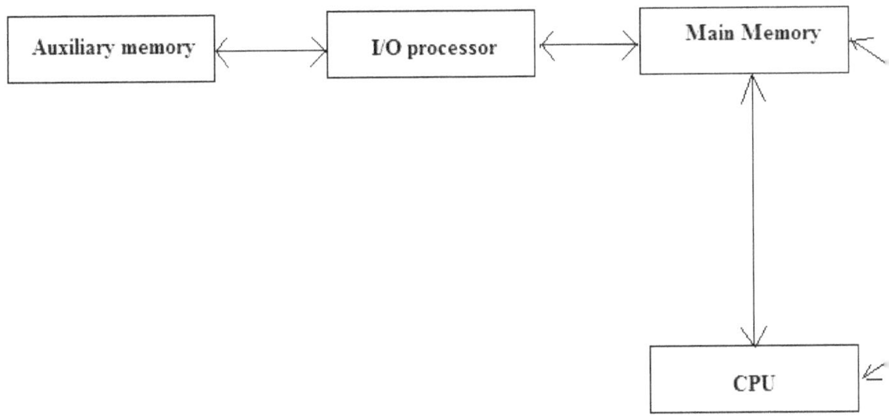

CPU logic is usually faster than main memory access time, with the result that processing speed is limited primarily by the speed of main memory. The cache is used for storing segments of programs currently being executed in the CPU and temporary data frequently needed in the present calculations. The typical access time ratio between cache and main memory is about 1to7. Auxiliary memory access time is usually 1000 times that of main memory

Memory Hierarchy

A memory system is a hierarchy of storage devices with different capacities, costs, and access times. A 'memory hierarchy' in computer storage distinguishes each level in the 'hierarchy' by response time. Since response time, complexity, and capacity are related, the levels may also be distinguished by the controlling technology. A 'memory hierarchy' in computer storage includes the Registers in CPU, Internal or Main memory which May include one or more levels of cache "RAM" and External memory for Backing store.

Memory Hierarchy is to obtain the highest possible access speed while minimizing the total cost of the memory system.

Most of the main memory in a general-purpose computer is made up of RAM integrated circuits chips, but a portion of the memory may be constructed with ROM chips. RAM– Random Access memory.

RAM has various types as explained below: --

Integrated RAM are available in two possible

operating modes, Static and Dynamic ROM– Read

Only memory

Static RAM (SRAM)

–   It is composed of 'cells'

- Retains value indefinitely, as long as it is kept powered – means as long as computer is "ON"

- This means that it is 'volatile' memory

- Faster and more expensive than DRAM

Dynamic RAM (DRAM)

- DRAM also has cells

- Each cell stores a bit

- Slower and cheaper than SRAM.

ROM is used for storing programs that are PERMANENTLY resident in the computer

- It is therefore non-volatile memory

- The ROM portion of main memory is needed for storing an initial program called bootstrap loader

- It is used while 'booting' a computer

  A RAM chip is better suited for communication with the CPU if it has one or more control inputs that select the chip when needed. The Block diagram of a RAM chip is shown in the slide, the capacity of the memory is 128 words of 8 bits (one byte) per word

  Memory Connection to CPU

- Memory Connection to CPU is Faster

- RAM and ROM chips are connected to a CPU through the data and address buses

- Bus is like wires connecting RAM & ROM to CPU

- This allows faster access

Summary-(In bullets)

- All computer perform the following basic operations for converting raw input data into useful information and presenting it to the user.

- A computer can process data, pictures, sound and graphics complicated problems quickly and accurately

- The storage unit of the computer holds data and instructions that are entered through the input unit, before they are processed

- <u>Primary storage:</u> stores and provides very fast access
- <u>Secondary storage</u> is used like an archive
- The size of the primary storage is specified in kb (kilobytes) or mb (megabyte). one kb is equal to 1024 bytes and one mb is equal to 1000kb.
- The output unit of a computer provides the information and results of a computation to outside world
- All calculations are performed in the arithmetic logic unit (alu) of the computer.
- Control unit: controls all other units in the computer.
- The control unit and alu of the computer are together known as the central processing unit (cpu).
- The memory unit that directly communicate with CPU is called the *main memory*
- The main memory occupies a central position by being able to communicate directly with the CPU and with auxiliary memory devices through an I/O processor
- CPU logic is usually faster than main memory access time, with the result that processing speed is limited primarily by the speed of main memory
- RAM– Random Access memory
- Integrated RAM are available in two possible operating modes, *Static and Dynamic*
- ROM– Read Only memory
- Static RAM (SRAM): Each cell stores bit with a six-transistor circuit.

- Dynamic RAM (DRAM): Each cell stores bit with a capacitor and transistor
- ROM is used for storing programs that are **PERMANENTLY resident** in the computer and for tables of constants that do not change in value once the production of the computer is completed
- RAM and ROM chips are connected to a CPU through the data and address buses

Self-assessment questions-(objective/subjective- minimum 5 questions)

1. CPU is like a_______________of computer
2. CPU consists of___&________
3. <u>Primary storage:</u> stores and provides very fast access (T/F?)

4. <u>Secondary storage</u> is used like an archive. What is other purposes of <u>Secondary storage</u>

5. Purpose of ALU is to_________________.

Chapter 1 Computer Block Diagrams

Introduction- The content of this unit introduces to the concept of Block Diagram of computer, which explains the main components of a computer. This unit will help the students to give insights on what exactly is inside a computer in general terms. For example, what are the building blocks of a computer is explained in this unit, along with examples.

Content-

A computer converts raw input data into useful information and presents it to the user in form of an output. Hence main components of the computer are Input, Processing and output as shown in the block diagram.

A detail of the block diagram is also shown in form of 5 parts – Input unit, Storage, Control unit, Arithmetic Logic Unit (ALU) and Output unit. This corresponds to the five basic operations performed by computer, which are: Inputting, Storing, Processing, Outputting &controlling. A computer can process data, pictures, sound and graphics complicated problems quickly and accurately. Computers need to receive data and instruction in order to solve any problem. Therefore, we need to input the data and instructions into the computers. The input unit consists of one or more input devices.

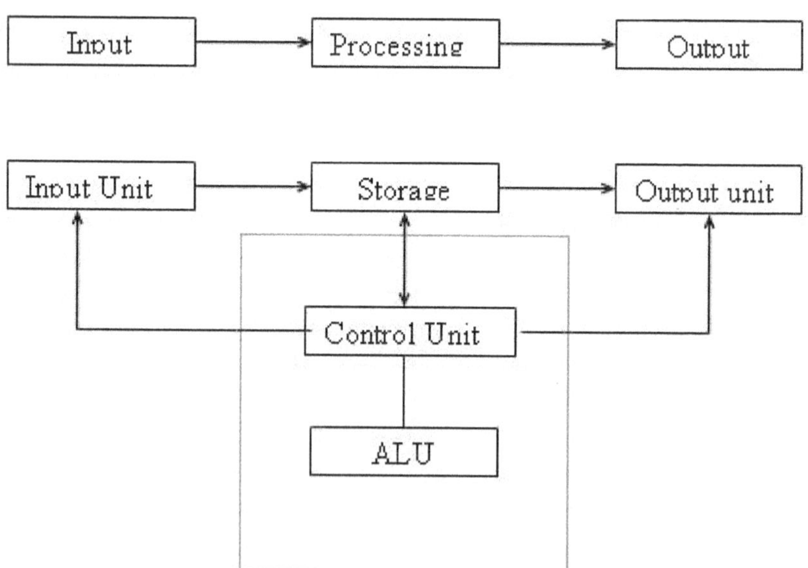

Figure: Block Diagram of a computer

Computers need to receive data and instruction in order to solve any problem. Therefore, we need to input the data and instructions into the computers. The input unit consists of one or more input devices. Keyboard is the one of the most commonly used input devices. Other commonly used input devices are the mouse, disk drives, magnetic tape, etc. <u>All the input devices perform the following functions</u>: Accept the data and instructions from the outside world, convert it to a form that the computer can understand. Supply the converted data to the computer system for further processing.

STORAGE UNIT: The storage unit of the computer holds data and instructions that are entered through the input unit, before they are processed. It preserves the intermediate and final results before these are sent to the output devices. It also saves the data for the later use.

Output Unit

The output unit of a computer provides the information and results of a computation to outside world.

Printers, Visual Display Unit (VDU) are the commonly used output devices.

<u>Other commonly used output devices are</u>

- ☐ floppy disk drive,

- ☐ hard disk drive, magnetic tape drive.

ARITHMETIC LOGICAL UNIT

All calculations are performed in the Arithmetic Logic Unit (ALU) of the computer.

It also does comparison and takes decision. The ALU can perform basic operations such as addition, subtraction, multiplication, division, etc and does logic operations like, $>$, $<$, $=$, 'etc. Whenever calculations are required, the control unit transfers the data from storage unit to ALU, once the computations are done, the results are transferred to the storage unit by the control unit and then it is send to the output unit for displaying results.

CONTROL UNIT

It controls all other units in the computer. The control unit instructs the input unit, where to store the data after receiving it from the user. It controls the flow of data and instructions from the storage unit to ALU. It also controls the flow of results from the ALU to the storage unit. The control unit is generally referred as the central nervous system of the computer that control and synchronizes its working.

CENTRAL PROCESSING UNIT

The control unit and ALU of the computer are together known as the Central Processing Unit (CPU).

The CPU is like brain performs the following functions:

- It performs all calculations.

- It takes all decisions.

- It controls all units of the computer.

A PC may have CPU-IC such as Intel 8088, 80286, 80386, 80486, Celeron, Pentium, Pentium Pro, Pentium II, Pentium III, Pentium IV, Dual Core, and AMD etc

Summary-(In bullets)

- All computer perform the following basic operations for converting raw input data into useful information and presenting it to the user.
- A computer can process data, pictures, sound and graphics complicated problems quickly and accurately
- The storage unit of the computer holds data and instructions that are entered through the input unit, before they are processed
- The output unit of a computer provides the information and results of a computation to outside world
- All calculations are performed in the arithmetic logic unit (alu) of the computer.
- Control unit: controls all other units in the computer.
- The control unit and alu of the computer are together known as the central processing unit (cpu).
- The memory unit that directly communicate with CPU is called the *main memory*

Self-assessment

questions-(objective/subjective-

minimum 5 questions) Fill in the

blanks:

1. CPU is like a_______________of computer:

a. Mind
b. Heart
c. Brain
d. head
2. CPU consists of___& ________
   a. Input & output
   b. Arithmetic & Logic
   c. ALU & Control Unit
   d. ALU & Logic Unit
3. Purpose of ALU is to________________.

   a. Process data

   b. Perform arithmetic and logic function

   c. Process input

   d. Process output

4. Building blocks of computer are______________:

    a. Input unit, processing unit & output unit

    b. Input, output and processor

    c. ALU & CPU

    d. Input & Output

5. Purpose of storage unit is to_________:

    a. Store data and instructions

    b. Store inputs

    c. Store outputs

    d. Store data

Chapter 2 - Memory Hierarchy

A memory system is a hierarchy of storage devices with different capacities, costs, and access

times. A 'memory hierarchy' in computer storage distinguishes each level in the 'hierarchy' by

response time. Since response time, complexity, and capacity are related, the levels may also be

distinguished by the controlling technology. A 'memory hierarchy' in computer storage includes

the Registers in CPU, Internal or Main memory which May

include one or more levels of cache "RAM" and External

memory for Backing store.

The memory unit is an essential component in any digital

computer since it is needed for storing programs and data. Not

all accumulated information is needed by the CPU at the same time.

Therefore, it is more economical to use low-cost storage devices to serve as a backup for storing the information that is not currently used by CPU.

The memory unit that directly communicate with CPU is called the main memory. Devices that provide backup storage are called auxiliary memory. The memory hierarchy system consists of all storage devices employed in a computer system from the slow by high- capacity auxiliary memory to a relatively faster main memory, to an even smaller and faster cache memory

The main memory occupies a central position by being able to communicate directly with the

CPU and with auxiliary memory devices through an I/O processor

A special very-high-speed memory called cache is used to increase the speed of processing by making current programs and data available to the CPU at a rapid rate. CPU logic is usually faster than main memory access time, with the result that processing speed is limited primarily by the speed of main memory. The cache is used for storing segments of programs currently being executed in the CPU and temporary data frequently needed in the present calculations. The typical access time ratio between cache and main memory is about 1to7. Auxiliary memory access time is usually 1000 times that of main memory.

Memory Hierarchy is to obtain the highest possible access speed while minimizing the total cost of the memory system. Most of the main memory in a general-purpose computer is made up of RAM integrated circuits chips, but a portion of the memory may be constructed with ROM chips.

RAM has various types as explained below: --

Integrated RAM are available in two possible
operating modes, Static and Dynamic ROM– Read
Only memory

Static RAM (SRAM)

– It is composed of 'cells'

– Retains value indefinitely, as long as it is kept powered – means as long as computer is "ON"

– This means that it is 'volatile' memory

– Faster and more expensive than DRAM

Dynamic RAM (DRAM)

– DRAM also has cells

– Each cell stores a bit

– Slower and cheaper than SRAM.

ROM is used for storing programs that are PERMANENTLY resident in the computer

– It is therefore non-volatile memory

–   The ROM portion of main memory is needed for storing an initial program called bootstrap loader

– It is used while 'booting' a computer

Summary-(In bullets)

The memory unit is an essential component in any digital computer

It is needed for storing programs and data

The memory unit that directly communicate with CPU is called the main memory The main memory occupies a central position by being able to communicate directly with the CPU and with auxiliary memory devices through an I/O processor

CPU logic is usually faster than main memory access time, with the result that processing speed is limited primarily by the speed of main memory

RAM– Random Access memory

Integrated RAM are available in two possible operating modes, Static and Dynamic ROM– Read Only memory

RAM and ROM chips are connected to a CPU through the data

and address buses

Self-assessment questions-(objective/subjective- minimum 5 questions)

1. Primary storage: stores and provides very fast access

a. True

b. False

2. Secondary storage is used like an archive

a. True

b. False

3. Purposes of Secondary storage is to:

a. Archive data

b. Provide storage to be used by CPU

c. Act as main memory

d. Act as RAM

4. CPU logic is usually_____than main memory access time.

a. Faster

b. Slower

5. Cache is

a. Primary memory

b. Main memory

c. Secondary memory

d. A special very-high-speed memory

Chapter 3 - CENTRAL PROCESSING UNIT (CPU)

Introduction- The content of this unit introduces to the CENTRAL PROCESSING UNIT (CPU) of computer, which explains this main component which controls a computer. It is part of one of the five basic operations performed by computer, which are: Inputting, Storing, Processing,

Outputting & controlling. The controlling operation is basically a part of CPU. In this unit the

object is to study the details of processing operations and controlling. Ample examples are given to explain this concept together with the help of a diagram,

Content-

CENTRAL PROCESSING UNIT (CPU) is the main component of the computer and its function is to control a computer. It is known that a computer converts raw input data into useful information and presents it to the user in form of an output. This corresponds to the five basic operations performed by computer, which are: Inputting, Storing, Processing, Outputting & controlling. The controlling operation is basically a part of CPU. Computers need to receive data and instruction in order to solve any problem. Therefore, we need to input the data and instructions into the computers. The input unit consists of one or more input devices. Keyboard is the one of the most commonly used input devices. Other commonly used input devices are the mouse, disk drives, magnetic tape, etc. All the input devices perform the following functions: Accept the data and instructions from the outside world, convert it to a form that the computer can understand. Supply the converted data to the computer system for further processing.

Figure: CPU Concept diagram

ARITHMETIC LOGICAL UNIT

All calculations are performed in the Arithmetic Logic Unit (ALU) of the computer.

It also does comparison and takes decision. The ALU can perform basic operations such as

addition, subtraction, multiplication, division, etc and does logic operations like, >, <, =, 'etc.

Whenever calculations are required, the control unit transfers the data from storage unit to ALU, once the computations are done, the results are transferred to the storage unit by the control unit and then it is send to the output unit for displaying results.

CONTROL UNIT

It controls all other units in the computer. The control unit instructs the input unit, where to store the data after receiving it from the user. It controls the flow of data and instructions from the storage unit to ALU. It also controls the flow of results from the ALU to the storage unit. The control unit is generally referred as the central nervous system of the computer that control and synchronizes its working.

CENTRAL PROCESSING UNIT

The control unit and ALU of the computer are together known as the Central Processing Unit (CPU).

The CPU is like brain performs the following functions:

• It performs all calculations.

• It takes all decisions.

• It controls all units of the computer.

Summary-(In bullets)

Control unit: controls all other units in the computer.

The control unit and alu of the computer are together

known as the central processing unit (cpu).

The memory unit that directly communicate with CPU is called
the main memory

The control unit and ALU of the computer are together

known as the Central Processing Unit (CPU)

The CPU is like brain performs the following functions:

o It performs all calculations.

o It takes all decisions.

o It controls all units of the computer.

Self-assessment

questions-(objective/subjective-

minimum 5 questions) Fill in the

blanks:

1. CPU is like a_______________of computer

a. Head of a computer

b. Brain of a computer

c. Heart of a computer

d. Mind of a computer

2. CPU consists of___& ________

a. Input & output

b. Arithmetic & Logic

c. ALU & Control Unit

a. ALU & Logic Unit

3. Purpose of ALU is to ________________

d. Process data

e. Perform arithmetic and logic function

f. Process input

g. Process output

4. The memory unit that directly communicate with CPU is called the

a. main memory

b. secondary memory

c. cache

d. storage

5. Control unit controls

a. all other units in the computer

b. Processing units in the computer

c. Input units in the computer

d. Output units in the computer

Chapter 4 - Introduction to logic gates

Introduction- The content of this unit Introduction to logic gates and related aspects as used in Digital Logic in a computer. This unit explains the concept of Logic gates that are actually electronic switches that process information. They are called gates because they open to produce a high output signal only when they receive the correct combination of input signals. Most logic gates have multiple inputs, which are used to determine a single output. A large number of logic gates can be incorporated in one

Content-

A Gate is a common structure we see every day and its purpose is to allow (or disallow) entry and exit. Similarly, we have the concept of Logic Gates.

Logic gates are electronic switches that process information. They are called gates because they open to produce a high output signal only when they receive the correct combination of input signals. Most logic gates have multiple inputs, which are used to determine a single output. A large number of logic gates can be incorporated in one electronic chip.

Digital systems have two states, ON and OFF. These simple electronic states are represented in binary code: ON is called logic 1; OFF is called logic 0. Microchips contain logic gates, which use this binary code to send and store information. Microchips can be easily damaged by high voltages. Due to this the voltages for the two logic states are standardized.

Logic 1 is 5 V, while logic 0 is 0 V.

Logic gates receive multiple signals in these two states. Different combinations of signals lead

to different outputs. There are mainly five types of gates – NOT, OR, AND, NOR & NAND.

NOT Gate has 1 input and 1 output. All other gates have two inputs and one output. There are mainly 5 types of logic Gates as shown below:

Some Tables for the Gates are shown below:

These tables show the inputs and output of the Gates and are self-explanatory.

Summary-(In bullets)

Logic gates are electronic switches that process information.

Digital systems have two states, ON and OFF.

These simple electronic states are represented in

binary code: ON is called logic 1; OFF is called

logic 0.

In a logic system both current and voltage are

very small to prevent damaging the gates.

This limits the range of output devices

which can be run on a logic system. There

are mainly five types of gates.

Self-assessment

questions-(objective/subjective-

minimum 5 questions) 1: What is a

Gate and what is its purpose?

a. Gate allows or disallows entry

b. Gate is used as it is a custom

c. Gate is used to secure a hour

d. Gate is used to enhance house structure

2: What is a Logic Gate and what is its purpose?

a.   they open to produce a high output signal only when they receive the correct combination of input signals

b. They are used to secure electronic circuits

c. They are used as it is custom just like we use doors or gates in a house

d.   Lo

gic gates

prevent

unauthoriz

ed access

3: List five

types of

Logic

Gates

a. AND, OR, NOT, NAND and NOR

b. AND, OR, NOT, NAND and NOTOR

c. AND, OR, NOT, NOTAND and NOR

d. AND, OR, NOT, ADD and MINUS

4. Digital systems have two states:

a. ON and OFF

b. PLUS and MINUS

c. ADD and SUBTRACT

d. NONE of the Above

5. Logic 1 is __V, while logic 0 is___V

a. 5 & 0

b. 1 & 0

c. 5 & -5

d. None of the above

Chapter 5 –Input and Output Devices

Introduction- The content of this unit introduces to the Input and Output Devices as used in a computer. This unit explains the concept of input and output devices, where the input devices translate data into a form that the system unit can process. Input devices convert what we understand into what the system unit can process. Output devices convert what the system unit has processed into a form that we can understand. Any data or instructions entered into a computer

Content-

Word Input is read and used many times but what is Input. Any data or instructions entered into a computer is regarded as input. Input devices translate data into a form that the system unit can process. Input devices convert what we understand into what the system unit can process. Output devices convert what the system unit has processed into a form that we can understand. Any data or instructions entered into a computer

Input devices translate data into a form that the system unit can process. Some hardware input

devices include: Keyboards, Mice, Pointing, Scanning, Image capturing & Audio-input.
Input

devices (key term) are hardware used to translate words,

sounds, images, nd actions that people understand into a form that the computer can understand. Input allows user to put their information into computer language. Most common are keyboard, mouse, scanning devices, image capturing devices and audio-input devices.

Keyboards (key term) come in a variety of designs – most common way to input data. Range from full-sized to miniature and from rigid to flexible

Common types

Traditional keyboard (key term) – full sized, rigid, rectangular keyboards that include function, navigational, and numeric keys

Laptop keyboard (key term) – used on laptop computers

Virtual keyboard (key term) – keyboard for a tablet PC and mobile devices– shown on a touch screen

Thumb keyboard

(key term) – used

on smartphones

Please refer to the

below diagram for

reference:

Pointing Devices (key term) provide an intuitive interface by

accepting pointing gestures and converting them into

machine-readable input. Pointing Devices provide an

intuitive

interface by accepting pointing gestures and converting

them into machine-readable input Wide variety of devices

such as: Mouse, Touch screen, Game controller, Stylus

Mouse (key term) controls a mouse pointer (key term) that

appears in the shape of an arrow. Some mice have a wheel

button (key term) for scrolling. The Optical Mouse (key term)

is the most widely used

Mouse types

Optical   mouse

(Key Term) – has

no moving parts

Emits and senses

light to detect mouse movement

Can be used on any surface

Cordless mouse (Key Term) or wireless mouse (Key Term) – battery powered Uses radio waves or infrared light waves

Touch pads (key term) –controls the pointer by moving and tapping your fingers on the surface of a pad

Output (key term) is process data or information. It converts machine-readable information into people-readable form. Most common output types – text, graphics, photos, audio, and

video. Output device (key term) is any hardware used to provide or to create output. The most widely used output devices (key term) are monitors, printer, and audio-output devices Monitors (key term) are commonly called display screens (Key Term)

Flat-Panel Monitors (key term) – are most widely used.
• Require less power to operate
• Portable and thin

• Most are backlit

See an example of Flat-bed monitor:

Printers (key term) translate information that has been processed by the system unit and present the information on paper

Speakers (key term) and headsets (key term) are the most widely used audio-output devices

Summary-(In bullets)

•   Input devices (key term) are hardware used to translate words, sounds, images, and actions that people understand into a form that the computer can understand

• Input allows user to put their information into computer language

•   Most common are keyboard, mouse, scanning devices, image capturing devices and audio-input devices

• Keyboards (key term) come in a variety of designs – most common way to input data

•   Pointing Devices (key term) provide an intuitive interface by accepting pointing gestures and converting them into machine-readable input

- Mouse (key term) controls a mouse pointer (key term) that appears in the shape of an arrow

- Output (key term) is process data or information

- Monitors (key term) are commonly called display screens (Key Term)

- Printers (key term) translate information that has been processed by the system unit and present the information on paper

Speakers (key term) and headsets (key term) are the most widely used audio-output devices

Self-assessment questions-(objective/subjective- minimum 5 questions)

1. Define input.

a. Any data entered into a computer is regarded as input.

b. Any instructions entered into a computer is regarded as input.

c. Any command entered into a computer is regarded as input.

d. Any data or instructions entered into a computer is regarded as input.

2. Define input devices.

a.   Input devices are software used to translate words, sounds, images, and actions that people understand into a form that the computer can understand

b.   Input devices are equipment used to translate words, sounds, images, and actions that people understand into a form that the computer can understand

c.   Input devices are modules used to translate words, sounds, images, and actions that people understand into a form that the computer can understand

d.   Input devices are hardware used to translate words, sounds, images, and actions that people understand into a form that the computer can understand

3. Describe keyboards.

a. Keyboards come in a variety of designs and most common way
   to input data

b. Keyboards come in a variety of designs and only way to input
   data

c. Keyboards come in single design and most common way to
   input data

d. Keyboards come in a single design and best way to input data

4. Describe pointing devices.

a.   provide an intuitive interface by accepting
pointing gestures and converting them into
machine-readable input

b.   provide an intuitive interface by accepting
pointing gestures and converting them into output.

c.   provide an intuitive interface by accepting
pointing gestures and converting them into pointers.

d.   provide an intuitive interface by accepting pointing gestures and converting them into machine language

5. Describe output.

a. Output is processed data

b. Output is processed information

c. Output is processed data or information

d. Output is processed input